AFOOT

AND LIGHTHEARTED

AFOOT

AND LIGHTHEARTED

A JOURNAL FOR MINDFUL WALKING

Bonnie Smith Whitehouse

Clarkson Potter/Publishers
New York

Published in the United States by Clarkson Potter/Publishers,
an imprint of the Crown Publishing Group, a division of
Penguin Random House LLC, New York.
crownpublishing.com
clarksonpotter.com

CLARKSON POTTER is a trademark and POTTER with colophon
is a registered trademark of Penguin Random House LLC.

ISBN 978-0-525-57481-1

Printed in China

Book and cover design by Danielle Deschenes
Cover and interior illustrations by Caitlin Keegan

10 9 8 7 6 5 4 3 2 1

First Edition

For Ben, Henry, and Peter—

HOW I LOVE SHARING THE TRAIL WITH YOU!

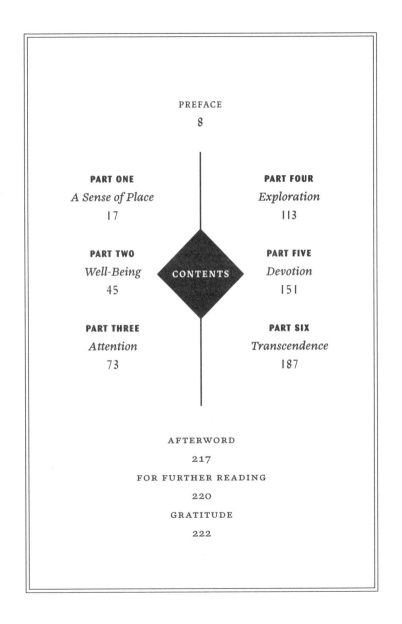

ALL TRULY GREAT
THOUGHTS ARE
CONCEIVED
WHILE WALKING.

—Friedrich Nietzsche

SOLVITUR AMBULANDO.

This ancient Latin phrase loosely translates as "It is solved by walking." A walk is a journey that requires very little—neither planning nor passport, neither ticket nor equipment. Nearly always at our disposal, a walk provides so much more than just a change of scenery. Walking has helped me decide what is wise and what is foolhardy, has made me fall in love with a place, has batted away my melancholy. Walking has helped me loosen the grip technology has on my life, giving me space and permission to disconnect from devices that beg for my attention and feed my anxiety. Most of all, walking has nurtured my creativity as I struggle to give tangible form to abstract ideas. And I'm not alone. A 2014 study by two Stanford researchers showed that a person's creative output increased by an average of 60 percent when walking.

This is an interactive journal, a book you are meant to carry with you and write in by hand. The only equipment you will need is your shoes and your pen. Given the fact that much of our life in the twenty-first century unfolds in front of screens, I hope you'll regard reading and using *Afoot and Lighthearted* as a countercultural activity. *Afoot and Lighthearted* is designed to help you discover the meaning of *solvitur ambulando* for yourself. For all who are captivated by the idea of learning a new way to cultivate mindfulness, walking provides the momentum that just might quiet your mind enough to inspire that sense of creativity you long to unearth or revive.

Every morning when I wake, I stretch my body from horizontal to vertical. I first walk to the kitchen, where I push the button on the coffeemaker. Second, I choose my next footpath. Will I walk to the nearest screen so that I may discover what fresh hell hath been wrought in the news overnight? Do I see what new claim on my attention shall be made by the emails that have accumulated while I slept? Or do I choose another path by slipping on some shoes and walking up the hill near my home that overlooks the city? Do I see who tweeted what, or do I watch the fat doves gather beneath the neighbors' bird feeders, pecking at the sunflower seeds that have fallen to the ground like raindrops? Each morning as I struggle with my overused attention, I will myself to take the latter path—to walk through the screened porch out into the morning air instead of losing myself in the glow of a screen. The walk is the path my heart prefers, but I freely admit it is not always the path I take.

I am never sorry when I choose the walk. I have walked miles on forest paths lined with purple larkspur with my college writing students. As a new mother, I have pushed a stroller up and down my neighborhood streets, letting the fresh air lull my son to sleep. When I couldn't stand to sit at my office desk any longer, I have walked laps around the perimeter of my university, planning the day's lessons in my head. A deliberate walk slows me down, quiets my mind, and stirs my senses.

Perhaps you long to experience for yourself how, all at once, walking can bring together your body, your mind, and the natural world. This book is designed to be an inspiring companion for those who'd like to use walking as a tool for heightening and training awareness, reviving energy, and cultivating a deeper sense of gratitude and creativity.

SO, WHAT'S
AFOOT AND LIGHTHEARTED
FOR ANYWAY?

Afoot and Lighthearted is a rejoinder to the demoralizing myth that the Goddess of Creativity strikes some lucky souls with her thunderbolt and leaves others behind. I know in my heart that creativity is for all, and we can all get more mindful when we walk. The title of this book embodies the action of mindful and creative walking and is a nod to Walt Whitman's celebrated poem "Song of the Open Road":

> Afoot and light-hearted I take to the open road,
> Healthy, free, the world before me,
> The long brown path before me leading wherever I choose.

> Henceforth I ask not good-fortune, I myself am good-fortune,
> Henceforth I whimper no more, postpone no more, need nothing,
> Done with indoor complaints, libraries, querulous criticisms,
> Strong and content I travel the open road.

—WALT WHITMAN, 1856

For decades, Walt Whitman's lines have echoed through my mind, teaching me that when we go afoot, we are invited to be "light-hearted," curious, and optimistic. Whitman—and so many others you'll learn about in *Afoot and Lighthearted*—used walking as a tool to revive creativity and refresh the imagination. Recent research from various fields shows that

12

time spent walking in nature can truly clarify thought and heighten creativity for us all. To take feet to ground is to take a brush to canvas. To take one step and then another is to compose the opening drum line. To take a walk is to discover enough clarity to create here, on this day. If you want to create, don't simply sit at a table or touch the screen—take a step out onto the earth.

Think of *Afoot and Lighthearted* as a map that will guide you onto a path that has been traveled by many mindful walkers before you, giving you the time, space, and permission to use the footpaths you have right outside your door to increase a sense of well-being and maybe a sense of creative freedom, too.

- **GRAB THIS BOOK, AND WALK AWAY!** Slip this portable journal into your bag and use it when you'd like to take a mindful walk at work, at school, or even while you're waiting for your morning coffee to brew. Use the prompts to propel yourself outdoors in natural or urban environments.

- **BEGIN ANYTIME, ANYWHERE, ON ANY PAGE.** *Afoot and Lighthearted* is organized around six themes: a sense of place, well-being, attention, exploration, devotion, and transcendence. Although you could certainly complete the prompts and activities in linear order from the book's beginning to end, *Afoot and Lighthearted* is designed so that you can easily skip around, completing a walk and prompt that appeals to you in the moment.

• **STRETCH YOUR PRACTICE, STRETCH YOUR MIND, AND STRETCH YOUR LEGS.** If you typically see yourself as a storyteller, prepare to sketch. If you are a painter or sculptor, prepare to use words to describe how the wind sounds as it comes across the water. If you are a runner, plan to discover walking afresh.

• **NO MATTER WHERE YOU LIVE, THIS BOOK IS FOR YOU.** Throughout *Afoot and Lighthearted*, I will frequently use the word *neighborhood* as a universal term for your direct surroundings, the immediate vicinity of the place you call home. Your neighborhood may have sidewalks, boardwalks, dirt trails, alleys, or fields. *Afoot and Lighthearted* is designed to be used by anyone in any sort of community, anywhere on earth.

AFOOT AND LIGHTHEARTED
IS FOR YOU IF

- **YOU WANT TO BE MORE PRESENT.** Perhaps you've heard a little about walking as a tool for mindfulness and you'd like to give it a try. If you find yourself preoccupied by thoughts of the past or thoughts of the future, reading and using *Afoot and Lighthearted* will bring you into the present moment.

- **YOU NEED TO EASE ANXIETY.** Perhaps you'd like to experience how your walking shoes can act as therapists, settling your anxieties and freeing up your mind as they propel you forward in space.

- **YOU LONG FOR MORE CREATIVITY IN YOUR LIFE.** Perhaps you already love to walk and appreciate the beauty of the natural world, and you long to get creative yourself.

- **YOU'D LIKE TO USE A WALK TO INCREASE PRODUCTIVITY.** Perhaps you're a creator or maker already, and you crave an excuse to step away from the screen or out of the studio into the fresh air.

- **YOU'RE IN NEED OF DIGITAL DETOX.** Perhaps the most light exposure you've had lately comes from your glowing screen, and you're desperately in need of sunshine, physical activity, and fresh air. If you find yourself constantly sidetracked by technology, this book is designed to help you improve your attention, your sense of focus, and your connection to place.

For many years, I have wondered how, in the frantic pace of this age we call our time, I might keep my focus on what nourishes me. I decided that, like many creative walkers before me, I had to disrupt habits that neither fed nor sustained me by radically and literally walking away from them. May this book help you walk toward a refuge of inner stillness you can always retreat to within yourself. This sort of refuge truly offers the "good-fortune" Whitman wrote about in "Song of the Open Road" so many years ago. And may *Afoot and Lighthearted* set you on an astonishing path toward abundance and creativity, a landscape you can traverse over and over for the rest of your days.

A Sense of Place

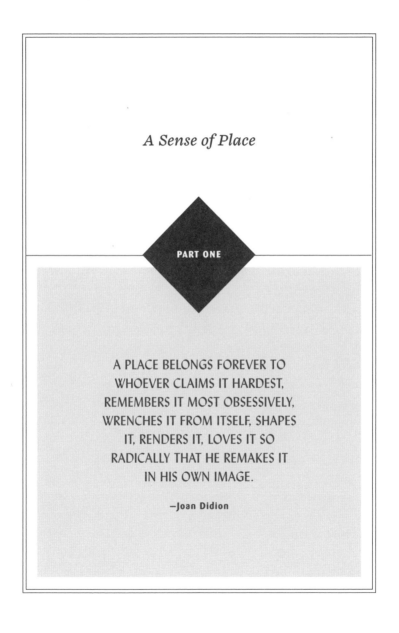

PART ONE

A PLACE BELONGS FOREVER TO
WHOEVER CLAIMS IT HARDEST,
REMEMBERS IT MOST OBSESSIVELY,
WRENCHES IT FROM ITSELF, SHAPES
IT, RENDERS IT, LOVES IT SO
RADICALLY THAT HE REMAKES IT
IN HIS OWN IMAGE.

—Joan Didion

Sitting before a glowing screen or behind the wheel of a car can make us feel as if we exist in a disembodied "no place." How better to reconnect with the earth and with our embodied existence than to go for a walk?

As I head out into my urban neighborhood, I always bend down to rub the mint growing beside the sidewalk between my thumb and forefinger, and when I bring my fingers up to my nose, the vigorous smell overpowers everything in my perception. The mint I planted is a descendant of the same mint my parents planted as newlyweds more than forty-five years ago at their first home. They have bought, renovated, or built five other homes over the course of their marriage, and steadfastly, they kept the same mint plant going from yard to yard, from garden to garden. My sister and I now tend progeny of that original mint plant. I can't walk by it without rubbing its leaves or picking off pieces to add to my tea and salads.

Like the mint I've imported from across the state, this street holds a history for our family; relatives of my husband bought a duplex on this lot after World War II. They lived in one side and rented the other side to family members or friends. I love to imagine that even though I never knew them, we have walked the same routes. For decades, my husband's mother kept that duplex as rental property. Ben lived there before we met, and soon after we married, we decided to tear down the well-worn home and build a modern one for our growing family so that we would be rooted on ancestral land. On the cold November afternoon the little duplex came down, we sat bundled up in fleece jackets in the yard across the street. Children from the neighborhood gathered and, with our little boys, danced and cheered when the demolition man's backhoe aggressively pierced the roof. As the bricks began tumbling to the ground, we felt that odd combination of both sorrow and delight; soon more heavy equipment arrived at the site to dig the basement and expose old roots and muddy earth. We are dug into this place; our mint roots spread wide, and our children run barefoot through sprinklers on the same earth where the great, great aunts and uncles they never knew walked.

This section of *Afoot and Lighthearted* is meant to help you identify and cultivate a sense of place as you walk. You will consider how places are bound by imaginary or real borders, and you will have the opportunity to play with analogies and experiment with music. Above all, you will be asked to develop or rekindle what writer Wendell Berry calls "affection for a place." When we walk consciously through a place, we establish a sense of our presence; the story of that place circulates through the consciousness. As we walk, our bodies join the history and the landscape. I hope you will go afoot and lighthearted to the open roads of your neighborhood and nurture a sense of place through mindful walking.

A NEIGHBORHOOD PILGRIMAGE

I am no scientist. I explore the neighborhood. An infant who has just learned to hold his head up has a frank and forthright way of gazing about him in bewilderment. He hasn't the faintest clue where he is, and he aims to learn. In a couple years, what he will have learned instead is how to fake it: He'll have the cocksure air of a squatter who has come to feel he owns the place. Some unwonted, taught pride diverts us from our original intent, which is to explore the neighborhood, view the landscape, to discover at least where it is that we have been so startlingly set down.

—Annie Dillard, *Pilgrim at Tinker Creek*

> No matter where you live, you have a neighborhood, and no matter how accustomed you are to its rhythms and idiosyncrasies, you still have much to learn from it.

◆ Set out on a walk around your neighborhood and pretend to see it as a tourist or newcomer might.

◆ With whom (or with what) do you share this piece of earth?

◆ How would you describe your landscape to others?

MY STREET

I am ten years old and I know every crack, bone and crevice in the crumbling sidewalk running up and down Randolph Street, my street. . . . On these streets I have been rolled in my baby carriage, learned to walk, been taught by my grandfather to ride a bike, and fought and run from some of my first fights. I learned the depth and comfort of real friendships, felt my early sexual stirrings and, on the evenings before air-conditioning, watched the porches fill up with neighbors seeking conversation and respite from the summer heat.

—Bruce Springsteen, *Born to Run*

◆ Think of a street that has held meaning for you, and walk there. Write about why that street has been important to you.

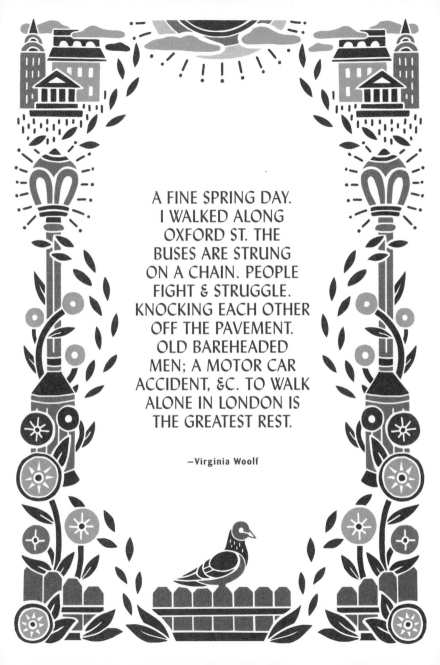

A FINE SPRING DAY.
I WALKED ALONG
OXFORD ST. THE
BUSES ARE STRUNG
ON A CHAIN. PEOPLE
FIGHT & STRUGGLE.
KNOCKING EACH OTHER
OFF THE PAVEMENT.
OLD BAREHEADED
MEN; A MOTOR CAR
ACCIDENT, &C. TO WALK
ALONE IN LONDON IS
THE GREATEST REST.

—Virginia Woolf

BORDERLINES

On this walk, consider the meaning of borders. Whether they are shorelines, property lines, neighborhood lines, the edges of a campus, or city limits, borders are fascinating.

◆ List the borders you see.

◆ Are the borders you see real or imaginary? What makes them so?

GLORIOUSLY IMPERFECT SKETCHES

I walk everywhere in the city. Any city. You see everything you need to see in a lifetime. Every emotion. Every condition. Every fashion. Every glory.

–Maira Kalman, *The Principles of Uncertainty*

◆ Grab your colored pens or pencils, set out on your walk. Stop and sketch the *emotions, conditions, fashions,* and *glories* you see in your neighborhood. Allow yourself to sketch without any need to make things "right" or "good." Perfection is not an option!

ANALOGIES

In 2014, Stanford University researchers Marily Oppezzo and Daniel L. Schwartz confirmed that walking increases creative ideation in real time, while the walker walks, and shortly after, when the walker stops. Specifically, they found that walking led to an increase in "analogical creativity" or using analogies to develop creative relationships between things that may not immediately look connected.

◆ Walk briskly for ten or fifteen minutes, and let your mind wander.

◆ Stop and make a list of ten to twenty things you've seen in the neighborhood. Number your list.

◆ Resume your walk, find a place to sit, and return to the list of things you've seen on your walk. See if you can find creative connections between pairs of items on your list.

AFFECTION

◆ Close your eyes and picture a nearby place for which you have affection. Write about why you love this place. Imagine sensory details: What sounds do you often *hear* there? What do you usually *see* when you go there? Is there a unique or compelling *feel* to the place?

◆ When you arrive, stop and look. Take notice of your senses. Return to your journal to record what you hear, see, and feel. Then make a list of other places you love and want to preserve.

MUSIC

What thrills me most about longleaf forests is how the pine trees sing. The horizontal limbs of flattened crowns hold the wind as if they are vessels, singing bowls, and air stirs in them like a whistling kettle. I lie in thick grasses covered with sun and listen to the music made there. This music cannot be heard anywhere else on the earth. Rustle, whisper, shiver, whinny. Aria, chorus, ballad, chant. Lullaby.

—Janisse Ray, *Ecology of a Cracker Childhood*

◆ Take a walk in a place that is sacred to you, and in the space below, use language to describe the music of that place.

SENSES

In a 2014 *New Yorker* article titled "Why Walking Helps Us Think," Ferris Jabr noted that a "small but growing collection of studies suggests that spending time in green spaces—gardens, parks, forests—can rejuvenate the mental resources that man-made environments deplete."

◆ Take a walk in a park, an arboretum, or a forest; by a lake; or in some other type of pastoral green space, and note how each of your senses responds.

ETERNITY

To see a World in a Grain of Sand
And a Heaven in a Wild Flower,
Hold Infinity in the palm of your hand
And Eternity in an hour.

—William Blake, "Auguries of Innocence"

◆ Walk out your front door and into your immediate
surroundings.

◆ Sit down and identify an object in your view (a rock, a flower,
a statue, a blade of grass, et cetera), and examine it in detail.

◆ Describe how this object might illuminate something beyond
the physical realm.

ARCADIA:
A PLACE OF PEACE AND HARMONY

Arcadia is a classical poetic ideal, a pastoral place that inspires harmony. Allow yourself to imagine an Arcadia, a place that lives in your history and your imagination, a place that brings you a sense of tranquility and peace just by thinking of it.

◆ Set out on a favorite walking route. After you've walked for fifteen minutes or so, find a place to sit and journal. Describe your Arcadia.

◆ Continue your walk and compare your current route with the Arcadia of your imagination. Stop to write about your thoughts or to sketch your Arcadia in your journal.

RETURNING FOR A PHOTOGRAPH

Flip back through the previous pages, and consider the physical relationship you've had with your neighborhood. Consider the object you found that held eternity or one of the borders you identified. Or consider a place in your neighborhood you attempted to view like a tourist or the "condition" or "glory" you tried to sketch.

◆ Walk back to the object, border, or place you've identified. Take several photographs of it, gather your belongings, and walk away.

◆ Walk for fifteen or twenty minutes, and attempt to clear your head.

◆ Find a place to sit, and choose one photograph to look at. Examine it side by side with your previous reflection, and write about the differences and similarities. If you like, draw a sketch of the photo to preserve it in your journal.

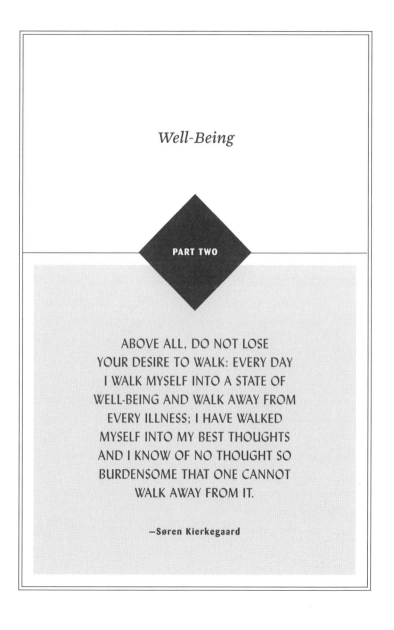

Well-Being

PART TWO

ABOVE ALL, DO NOT LOSE
YOUR DESIRE TO WALK: EVERY DAY
I WALK MYSELF INTO A STATE OF
WELL-BEING AND WALK AWAY FROM
EVERY ILLNESS; I HAVE WALKED
MYSELF INTO MY BEST THOUGHTS
AND I KNOW OF NO THOUGHT SO
BURDENSOME THAT ONE CANNOT
WALK AWAY FROM IT.

—Søren Kierkegaard

At my university, I lead an interdisciplinary course on walking, writing, and well-being. Over the years, hundreds of thoughtful, kindhearted students have passed through my class, often opening my eyes to the problematic ways we humans divide ourselves. As an obvious example, we carve human knowledge into categories like "literature" or "science," and these divisions can seriously limit our understanding of the vastness of human experience. Many of us also inherit an assumption that treats "mind" as distinct from "body," and "feeling" as separate from "thinking." Noticing these tendencies in my students, I have learned that walking is a gentle way to push ourselves to reconsider these dualistic assumptions and begin to more fully integrate body and mind.

Did you know that taking a short brisk walk—even for only twenty minutes per day—can reduce the risk of heart disease, Alzheimer's, depression, diabetes, and several types of cancer? In addition, research has shown that expressive writing (especially about emotional experiences) can boost immune function and lower stress. So, compelling evidence suggests that combining regular walking with a consistent journaling practice can make us healthier, happier, and less stressed.

Getting outside and going for a walk has long been considered a remedy for the physical and mental afflictions that ail us. Back in 1901, in an essay on America's national parks, writer and environmental activist John Muir declared, "Thousands of tired, nerve-shaken, over-civilized people are beginning to find out that going to the mountains is going home; that wildness is a necessity; and that mountain parks and reservations are useful not only as fountains of timber and irrigating rivers, but as fountains of life." Muir might have been anticipating the needs of our time.

We can't all drop everything and retreat "home" to the mountains, but we can lace up our shoes and seek out fountains of health by taking walks in our neighborhoods. The prompts in this section will show you how you can walk yourself into an improved sense of well-being in creative ways that might surprise you.

Resist the temptation to think of well-being as something we can only cultivate within ourselves as individuals. I hope this section will encourage you to think of the well-being of your community and nation as well as your own personal well-being.

WALKING FOR HEALTH

I have two doctors, my left leg and my right.

—G. M. Trevelyan

> Walking has long been a pastime in the United
> Kingdom. In the mid-1990s, Britain's National Health
> Service started recommending health walks to
> encourage citizens to be active, which eventually led
> to the formation of a national program of organized
> communal rambles. The weekly walks boost physical
> and mental well-being, as well as help people build
> social networks.

◆ Set out on a walk, and consider the common beliefs about
health in your nation.

◆ In your journal, consider whether you think walking is tied
to your understanding of yourself as a citizen of a particular
nation. As a citizen of the world?

◆ As you continue your walk, brainstorm the connections
between walking, well-being, and citizenship.

YOU, EMBODIED

[An] ancient error was to divide between body and feeling, then again between feeling and thinking. . . . The body ended up at the bottom, as if it were the least human "part" of us, as if it could be safely given over to the mechanists without our thereby losing feeling and thought. It isn't so.

—Eugene T. Gendlin, *Thinking Beyond Patterns: Body, Language, and Situations*

> Human beings are not neatly divided into bodies and minds; we walk through this world as embodied beings. Our bodies contain, feel, and think; our bodies make creation possible.

◆ Write or sketch an answer to the following: How might you— a creative, embodied self—connect with the creativity your body inherently possesses by doing something as simple as writing by hand?

◆ Are there other ways you can live so that you aren't caught up in the ancient divides Gendlin describes above?

SOME PEOPLE HAVE SAID THERE'S
A RELATIONSHIP BETWEEN POETIC
METER AND THE FALL OF YOUR
FOOT—AND POSSIBLY YOUR
HEARTBEAT MIGHT BE THOUGHT
OF AS AN IAMBIC BEAT WHEN IT'S
AMPLIFIED BY WALKING. OFTEN
WHEN I GO FOR A WALK I COME
BACK WITH A POEM. THERE'S A
SENSE OF CREATIVITY ABOUT IT,
AND A SENSE OF WELLBEING THAT
YOU ARE GETTING THE ORGANS
AND LUNGS AND THE BLOOD
MOVING. YOU NEVER COME BACK
FROM A WALK FEELING WORSE.

—Simon Armitage

TECH SABBATH

Many of us live in two worlds. First, we live in the physical world where we see the sunlight shimmering and feel silky blades of grass between our fingers. But we also live in the virtual world displayed on our smartphone screens, where our brains get caught up in dopamine-fueled reward loops of anticipating, checking, and receiving information.

Why not give yourself the gift of a tech sabbath and block off the digital world for a day?

◆ Put aside screens for twenty-four hours. Be unavailable except to those who are closest to you.

◆ Take a long walk in the middle of your tech sabbath, carrying only your journal. Consider the scenery and the physical world to which you belong. Consider your social life and your interactions with people close to you and people you've never met. Consider your waking and sleeping habits.

◆ Take some time to reflect on how technology affects your overall sense of well-being.

FOREST BATHING

Developed in Japan in the 1980s, *shinrin-yoku*
translates as "taking in the forest atmosphere"
or "forest bathing" and draws on the forest as a
site for healing. Not to be mistaken for hiking or
a nature walk, *shinrin-yoku* is a way of savoring
the forest atmosphere. The point of *shinrin-yoku* is
to "bathe" or luxuriate in nature for several hours.

◆ Find a forested green space, and leave your cell phone behind.
It's important that *shinrin-yoku* takes place in a setting where
you can soak up the sensory details of the woods.

◆ Breathe deeply, be silent, slow down, and meditate on your
surroundings.

◆ Go barefoot, and give yourself permission to stop in an
appealing place and lie down on the ground.

◆ Make an effort to engage all of your senses, and imagine
you are bathing in the atmosphere of your surroundings,
breathing in the aroma of the forest.

◆ Notice your lightened mood and a heightened sense of clarity,
connectedness, and creativity. Take time to write or sketch
about your *shinrin-yoku* experience.

BETWEEN
EVERY TWO
PINE TREES
THERE IS
A DOOR

LEADING TO A NEW WAY OF LIFE.

—JOHN MUIR

GRATITUDE

Gratitude is not only the greatest of virtues, but the parent of all others.

—Marcus Tullius Cicero

> Journaling and taking a walk specifically devoted to expressing gratitude merges three powerful tools for boosting well-being. Psychology researcher Robert Emmons has found that people who keep gratitude journals exercise more regularly, have fewer physical complaints, and generally feel better about their lives. He has also noted that thankful people cope better with stress and tend to have lower levels of depression.

◆ Take a walk in which you focus on gratitude: What are you grateful for? Who or what has made that possible? Have you overlooked it in any way?

◆ Focus on one particular person whom you'd like to thank, and write a letter to that person expressing your gratitude.

BLESSED ARE THEY WHO
SEE BEAUTIFUL THINGS IN
HUMBLE PLACES WHERE
OTHERS SEE NOTHING.

—Camille Pissarro

SEEK GOOSE BUMPS

One cannot but be in awe when one contemplates the mysteries of eternity, of life, of the marvelous structure of reality. It is enough if one tries merely to comprehend a little of this mystery each day. Never lose a holy curiosity.

—Albert Einstein

> To experience awe is to experience astonishment, a sense of the sublime, a feeling of the vastness of the universe that you don't entirely comprehend. Sometimes awe can come when we witness something physical (like the dizzying view from the top of a skyscraper) or perceptual (like a magnificent painting). Researchers have even found that experiencing awe is linked to better health!

◆ How might you go out of your way to seek awe?

◆ Walk to a place that is somewhat new to you—a cathedral, a mountaintop, an art museum—or venture to the top of a skyscraper. Or make time to witness a sunrise, a sunset, or starlight.

◆ Write a brief poem about what it felt like to seek awe.

IF I HAD INFLUENCE WITH
THE GOOD FAIRY WHO IS
SUPPOSED TO PRESIDE OVER
THE CHRISTENING OF ALL
CHILDREN I SHOULD ASK THAT
HER GIFT TO EACH CHILD IN THE
WORLD BE A SENSE OF WONDER
SO INDESTRUCTIBLE THAT IT
WOULD LAST THROUGHOUT LIFE,
AS AN UNFAILING ANTIDOTE
AGAINST THE BOREDOM
AND DISENCHANTMENTS OF
LATER YEARS, THE STERILE
PREOCCUPATION WITH ALL
THINGS ARTIFICIAL, THE
ALIENATION FROM THE SOURCES
OF OUR STRENGTH.

—Rachel Carson

WALKING FOR THE WELL-BEING OF OTHERS

Before cars and bicycles were mass-produced and readily available, walking was the main way humans got from place to place. These days it seems as if we have to go out of our way to walk. Sidewalks disappear. Cars often seem more welcome in many of our cities than pedestrians, and we tend to accept this without even thinking about what it means for the body and the imagination.

And yet data informs us that walkability benefits creativity and public health, and can lead to more connected, enfranchised communities.

◆ Learn your community's walk score by consulting walkscore.com.

◆ Research an organization advocating for more walkability in your area.

IF YOU
DEVELOP A
STRONG SENSE
OF CONCERN
FOR THE
WELL-BEING OF
ALL SENTIENT
BEINGS . . . ,

THIS WILL
MAKE YOU
HAPPY IN
THE MORNING.
EVEN *BEFORE*
COFFEE.

—THE DALAI LAMA

Attention

PART THREE

THE BRAIN—
IS WIDER THAN THE SKY—

—Emily Dickinson

On a wall in my office, I have a framed needlepoint piece that reads, "I know I'm efficient. Tell me I'm beautiful." I find both sparkling wit and profound wisdom in those two sentences. I first imagine them as the lines an exhausted woman vents to her partner at the end of the day. But then I wonder if those eight words are being spoken to me by Existence itself, imploring me to worry less about productivity and give my attention instead to the magnificence that surrounds me.

When it comes to mastering the art of paying attention, I freely admit that I am a work in progress. Is it an accepted truth that the things that irritate you most about others are really the things that most deeply frustrate you about yourself? If so, paying attention may be that trait for me. When I witness those I work with or those I love giving their attention to tablets or cell phones instead of the people standing in front of them, I feel so annoyed. My default response is to empathize with the overlooked person, imagining the sting of being unseen. But if I'm honest, my frustration is really directed inward at my own ongoing struggle to be attentive and present in a world full of distracting curiosities.

Many years ago, I read Alice Walker's novel *The Color Purple,* and one line has echoed through my head for decades, serving as both a reminder and a chastisement of the me who often isn't paying attention: "I think it pisses God off if you walk by the color purple in a field somewhere and don't notice it." I desperately want to be one who pays close attention; I don't want to sleepwalk through this beautiful world and miss the color purple putting on a show beside my footpath.

But how easy it can be to get distracted by that cobweb developing on the windowsill, an unsightly blight that simply must be eradicated at once because having a clean home is *virtuous*. Or instead, how I can mindlessly plan what needs to happen in the next hour so that I can complete my list because doing so demonstrates my *competence*. Needing to establish that I am virtuous because my home is clean or I am competent because my tasks are completed is a bit of a trap if I want to live my life with presence, joy, and creativity.

In *Your Creative Brain*, psychologist Shelley Carson suggests the importance of maintaining strict boundaries between our "absorb states" (thinking, taking in new ideas) and our "synthesis states" (executing the new ideas). When we spend time in the absorb state, we are refreshing our attention; our minds are more playful and open to ideas. In the synthesis state, our minds are ready to carry out ideas; this is the time to sit down at the desk or even on the trail to work.

In this section, you'll learn about how walks can harness your attention and make you more mindful of your surroundings. When we imitate masters like Beethoven, Nietzsche, and Mary Oliver by integrating regular walks into our routines, we can absorb the landscape and establish a sense of presence in our bodies. The fatigue we may feel after a walk can bring a sense of peace, and in that peace, the attention is refreshed, focused, and present. We're less likely to miss the color purple.

NAME YOUR RABBIT TRAILS

The Net is, by design, an interruption system, a machine geared for dividing attention. . . . We willingly accept the loss of concentration and focus, the division of our attention and the fragmentation of our thoughts, in return for the wealth of compelling or at least diverting information we receive.

—Nicholas Carr, *The Shallows*

> For so many of us, the digital age is a double-edged sword full of both wondrous curiosities and continuous rabbit trails of distractions. Give your overused attention a break.

◆ As you walk, stay mindful of your surroundings and of the present moment, without slipping into thoughts of the past or the future, or of anything that's not in your current sensory experience. As you walk, tally and name any distractions that arise.

◆ Write about why you find the distractions so alluring. Are these rabbit trails simply pleasurable excursions of the mind? Or are they about your fears or anxieties?

A TURN OR TWO I'LL WALK,
TO STILL MY BEATING
MIND.

—Prospero,
The Tempest, **4.1**

RISE AND REFLECT
WITH FRIEDRICH NIETZSCHE

The great philosopher Friedrich Nietzsche composed much of his work on foot and in absolute solitude. He was especially drawn to strenuous mountain paths beside glorious bodies of water. French philosopher Frédéric Gros argues that the landscape truly shaped the quality and content of Nietzsche's work; because Nietzsche wrote *while* he walked in stunning dramatic scenery, his writing was more daring and profound.

◆ Give your attention to a tough question while you venture onto a challenging footpath that includes some elevation, raises your heart rate, and makes you breathe hard.

◆ Write your tough question here:

◆ Contemplate your question as you walk, and imitating Nietzsche, catch your breath on the trail, and take some time to journal in response to your question.

MY EXPERIENCE IS WHAT I AGREE TO ATTEND TO.

ONLY THOSE ITEMS WHICH I NOTICE SHAPE MY MIND.

—WILLIAM JAMES

IDLENESS IS GLORIOUS

Despite all the signals we receive from our culture, we don't have to feel guilty if we're not always rushing or learning or doing. In fact, boredom, rest, and idleness can be profound ways to stimulate the imagination and let our attention expand and unfurl.

◆ Embrace the merits of boredom by walking for absolutely no reason at all.

◆ When you feel your mind relax and unwind, find a place on your route to sit and write or sketch.

NOW, MY TREE-CLIMBING DAYS LONG BEHIND ME, I OFTEN THINK ABOUT THE LASTING VALUE OF THOSE EARLY, DELICIOUSLY IDLE DAYS. I HAVE COME TO APPRECIATE THE LONG VIEW AFFORDED BY THOSE TREETOPS. THE WOODS WERE MY RITALIN. NATURE CALMED ME, FOCUSED ME, AND YET EXCITED MY SENSES.

—Richard Louv

CATCH WONDER

When laughing children chase after fireflies, they are not pursuing beetles, but catching wonder. When wonder matures, it peels back experiences to seek deeper layers of marvel below.

—David George Haskell, *The Forest Unseen: A Year's Watch in Nature*

> In *The Forest Unseen*, David George Haskell records—over the course of a year—his visits to a randomly chosen circle about a yard in diameter. Though Haskell is a biologist, his purpose was not to conduct experiments or do research on this little spot of land; his purpose was to watch and listen to that which is frequently unseen, taking only binoculars, a magnifying glass, and a notebook.

◆ Take your journey to find a little circle of earth to visit. "Catch wonder" by observing, appreciating, and marveling at the often-unseen life teeming all around you.

WALK AFTER LUNCH LIKE BEETHOVEN

Part of Ludwig van Beethoven's creative routine included a planned walk each day after lunch. This daily walk in the woods was an important part of his composing process, a way he was able to separate his work environment (or what psychologists call the synthesis state) from his thinking environment (the absorb state).

◆ Integrate a walk into your routine to create a little momentum and a literal way to walk away from too much sensory stimulation.

◆ **START SMALL:** Shorten your lunch period by ten minutes for the next five days, and use those ten minutes to walk. Briefly record your observations here.

DAY ONE

DAY TWO

DAY THREE

DAY FOUR

DAY FIVE

I CAN ONLY MEDITATE
WHEN I AM WALKING,
WHEN I STOP I CEASE TO
THINK; MY MIND ONLY
WORKS WITH MY LEGS.

—Jean-Jacques Rousseau

WALK AND TALK

Today's worker is often much too sedentary; walking meetings are wonderful ways to get out of our chairs, connect with colleagues, and brainstorm new ideas in the fresh air. Walking meetings have found advocates among those who like to move their bodies, step away from distracting emails, and engage in a focused, creative conversation.

◆ Prepare for a walking meeting by writing down three or four items you want to make sure you discuss:

1. _____

2. _____

3. _____

4. _____

◆ Where did you go?

◆ How did your walking meeting differ from a traditional meeting, particularly when it comes to attention, listening, creativity, and brainstorming?

I AM
ALARMED
WHEN IT
HAPPENS
THAT I HAVE
WALKED A
MILE INTO
THE WOODS
BODILY,

WITHOUT GETTING THERE IN SPIRIT.

—HENRY DAVID THOREAU

I WILL TELL YOU WHAT
I HAVE LEARNED ABOUT
MYSELF. FOR ME, A LONG
FIVE- OR SIX-MILE WALK
HELPS. AND ONE MUST GO
ALONE AND EVERY DAY.

—Brenda Ueland

THOREAU'S PATHWAYS

As a single footstep will not make a path on the earth, so a single thought will not make a pathway in the mind. To make a deep physical path, we walk again and again. To make a deep mental path, we must think over and over the kind of thoughts we wish to dominate our lives.

—from the journal of Henry David Thoreau

> The rabbit trails of distraction don't have to govern our days and become well-worn grooves in our minds. Take a long walk, and as Thoreau suggests, deliberately turn your mind to positive thinking. Think of this walk as an opportunity to orient yourself—and the pathways in your brain—on the deeper path you truly want to tread.

◆ Choose a particular word, mantra, or credo you "wish to dominate" your life, and bring your attention there as you walk.

◆ Write the word, mantra, or credo here and turn it into an inspirational banner or badge you might see in an artist's studio or at your own desk.

BE WHERE
YOUR FEET ARE.

—Traditional

WALKING MEDITATION I

When you practice walking meditation, you simply bring your attention and awareness to each step you take. Mindfulness expert Jon Kabat-Zinn encourages us to use walking as a mindfulness tool, so that we may "therefore transform it from a dull, mostly unconscious chore into something rich and nurturing."

◆ Find a straight, simple path. You may choose to walk barefoot to increase sensation at the soles of your feet.

◆ As you walk, notice what your heels, arches, and, finally, your toes feel like as they meet the ground. If your mind wanders, bring it back to noticing sensations.

I
SHUT
MY
EYES

IN ORDER TO SEE.

—PAUL GAUGUIN

ATTENTION:
THE BEGINNING OF DEVOTION

Mary Oliver, a contemporary poet and essayist, has written, "My work is loving the world." Oliver contends that she simply *must* walk each and every day to generate ideas and carry out her mission to love and attend to our physical world. She provocatively claims that "attention is the beginning of devotion."

◆ Walk for ten minutes before stopping to make a list of the things you tend to pay attention to in life. Consider the contents of your list and this question: What if the job description of a human being on this planet is simply to pay attention?

◆ Consider how your attention leads to your devotion. Is your attention leading to the things in life you want to be devoted to?

◆ Return to Oliver's original claim that her "work is loving the world." What would you say your work is?

HOW WE SPEND OUR
DAYS IS, OF COURSE,
HOW WE SPEND OUR
LIVES. WHAT WE DO WITH
THIS HOUR AND WITH
THAT ONE, IS WHAT WE
ARE DOING.

—Annie Dillard

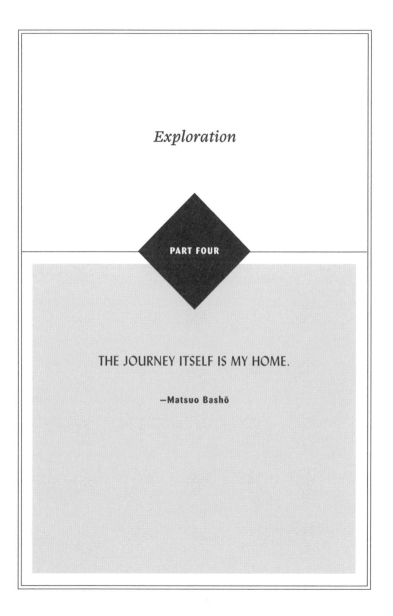

Exploration

PART FOUR

THE JOURNEY ITSELF IS MY HOME.

—Matsuo Bashō

To explore is to delight in taking a risk, and I have two items in my possession that frequently remind me of this truth. First, a paperweight given to me many years ago by a beloved friend: on it is engraved the question "What would you attempt to do if you knew you could not fail?" Some mornings, I run my fingers over the words, trying to imagine how I might answer it on that particular day. Where might I go if I could remove the dread of disappointment from the equation of my hours? What might I make? The fear of failure—or really, the fear of the unknown— can weigh down creative work like an albatross.

The second, a book given to me by a college roommate: a copy of *Life Doesn't Frighten Me*, Maya Angelou's sassy and intrepid poem, brilliantly illustrated by the bold graffiti artist Jean-Michel Basquiat. When she gave me this book, my friend said that Angelou's unflinching poem reminded her of *me*, a claim that shocked me down to my marrow because I considered myself full of fear. But the astonishing knowledge that someone else regarded me as brave infused me with a shot of courage, allowing me to step into adventures with more heart and less fear.

The pathless wood, the blank page, the empty canvas, the silence awaiting a chord: these are all new territories to explore. When we compose and create without fearing the eventual outcome, we become pioneers of the unknown. As you set out on the trail and encounter the following prompts, consider the practice of freewriting, a creative technique advocated by marvelous teachers like Peter Elbow, Julia Cameron, and Natalie Goldberg. When we freewrite, we write or sketch for a determined amount of time without stopping, erasing, editing, or revising. Our pens stubbornly journey on, even when we are unsure where to take them. Try very hard to silence your inner critic as you journal without stopping for, say, a ten- or twenty-minute period. Freewriting is playful and gratifying, like taking your pen on a joyride with no map, no path, and a full tank of gas (of ink!).

The following prompts will lead you on trails through an urban landscape and on journeys emulating adventurer-artists like Charles Dickens and Cheryl Strayed. Like freewriting, exploring on foot can be generative and delightful. To explore is to discover new worlds but also to experiment, to play, to amble without purpose, and to dwell in awareness without focusing on any particular thing. At the heart of exploratory walks is an eager willingness to abide in unknowing.

NOW SHALL I WALK OR SHALL I RIDE?

"RIDE," PLEASURE SAID;

"WALK," JOY REPLIED.

—W. H. DAVIES

A WANDERING PENCIL

[A drawing is] an active line on a walk, moving freely, without goal. A walk for a walk's sake.

—Paul Klee

◆ Take a walk with no destination in mind. Instead, simply meander and explore. Upon your return, make a dot, to mark the start of your walk. Draw a continuous line representing your meandering walk. Embellish your drawing with labels or illustrations, creatively mapping the path you wandered.

EXPLORING THE STACKS

Knowledge sets us free, art sets us free. A great library is freedom.

—Ursula Le Guin, *The Wave in the Mind*

> Public libraries are fertile soil for creativity; they
> belong to us all and are a communal good. Walk to
> your public library, and when you arrive, wander
> through the stacks. Collect books from any genre
> that calls out to you—biographies, essays, children's
> books, histories, periodicals, novels, art books,
> poetry. Have a seat in the library and pore over
> your collection.

◆ Write about a new path you're discovering in these books
you've found.

◆ Or take a cue from Le Guin and begin writing, "This is what
set me free: _____," and see where you
are led.

AS YOU START TO
WALK OUT ON THE WAY,
THE WAY APPEARS.

—Rumi

A NIGHT WALK

I cannot walk through the suburbs in the solitude of night without thinking
that night pleases us because it suppresses idle details, just as our memory
does.

—Jorge Luis Borges, "A New Refutation of Time"

◆ Step away from all idle details and head out into the night,
walking in the dark along a path you already know well. If
you'd like, take a human companion or a furry friend. Pay extra
attention to what your senses are telling you about the night.
Observe the difference in sounds, sights, and temperature. On
your night walk, allow yourself time and space to stargaze, to
wonder, and to delight in the evening's gifts.

RACEWALKERS AND VAGABONDS

My walking is of two kinds: one, straight on end to a definite goal at a round pace; one, objectless, loitering, and purely vagabond. In the latter state, no gipsy on earth is a greater vagabond than myself.

—Charles Dickens, *The Uncommercial Traveller*

> Many are surprised to learn that the mid-nineteenth century was the era of "pedestrianism," or race-walking, and one of the sport's most well-known participants was Charles Dickens. Creative work didn't come fast and easy to Dickens, but walking did. He often bolted from his writing desk for a twenty-mile walk through London's streets and suburbs, considering himself a vagabond.

◆ Use your own pedestrian abilities to lift a creative block. Walk as long, fast, and far as you can today.

◆ Journal about how we are all descended from vagabonds and rebels.

I WOULD WALK ALONG
THE QUAIS WHEN I HAD
FINISHED WORK OR
WHEN I WAS TRYING TO
THINK SOMETHING OUT.
IT WAS EASIER TO THINK
IF I WAS WALKING AND
DOING SOMETHING OR
SEEING PEOPLE DOING
SOMETHING THAT THEY
UNDERSTOOD.

—Ernest Hemingway

THE FLANEUR AND
THE URBAN LANDSCAPE

The French concept of the flaneur, which comes
from nineteenth-century literature, has no correlation
in English. The flaneur takes a step back from
hustling and bustling through the city and decides
simply to stroll or saunter in the midst of the crowd,
idly exploring the urban landscape. There is no
specific destination the flaneur has in mind; his only
goal is to practice the art of idle observation in the
midst of busyness.

◆ Walk in an urban environment for ten minutes, practicing
the flaneur's art of strolling among the crowd. Freewrite in
your journal about the experience.

◆ Walk with purpose and speed for the next ten minutes.
Get your heart rate up, and try to stay ahead of the crowd.

◆ Reflect in your journal on the difference between the two.

"BECAUSE I WANTED TO"

In 1955, at age sixty-seven, Emma Gatewood of Ohio let her family know she was going to take a walk. Wearing a pair of Keds sneakers, Grandma Gatewood (as she was affectionately called) set off, carrying an army blanket, a raincoat, and a shower curtain to protect her from the elements—and hiked the 2,050 miles of the Appalachian Trail alone.

Her reasons for choosing this path seemed to be escape and adventure. For more than thirty years, she had been abused by her husband in a time when battered women were often not protected by the law. Grandma Gatewood set out on that first long walk to claim her own life after reading a *National Geographic* article about the Appalachian Trail, and she became the first woman to hike the trail alone. When asked why she originally decided to set out on this trek, Grandma Gatewood said, "Because I wanted to."

◆ Imagine you're near the end of your life and being interviewed about something wild and adventuresome you once did. What would that be? Journal a few paragraphs beginning with the sentence, "I _____ because I wanted to."

WALKING, IN PARTICULAR
DRIFTING, OR STROLLING,
IS ALREADY—WITH THE
SPEED CULTURE OF
OUR TIME—A KIND OF
RESISTANCE . . . A VERY
IMMEDIATE METHOD FOR
UNFOLDING STORIES.

—Francis Alÿs

I'VE BEEN
ABSOLUTELY
TERRIFIED
EVERY
MOMENT
OF MY
LIFE

AND I'VE NEVER LET IT KEEP ME FROM DOING A SINGLE THING THAT I WANTED TO DO.

—ATTRIBUTED TO GEORGIA O'KEEFFE

OUTDOOR INCLUSION

We are changing the visual narrative, and inspiring access to the most pristine nature as well as urban nature, including local parks, trails, and open spaces. These activities promote not only a healthy lifestyle, they also help communities find healing, connect to black history found in many natural areas, and inspire an increased desire to protect vulnerable public lands for all to enjoy.

—from the agenda of Outdoor Afro

> The National Park Service currently estimates that just 7 percent of the people who explore America's national parks are black. Outdoor Afro is a network seeking to change this narrative by making conservation, exploration, and outdoor experiences more inclusive.

◆ Walk a new path today and journal about the legacy you've inherited: What attitudes and beliefs did your family hold about exploration, particularly when it came to exploring wild, wooded, or unknown spaces?

PATHS ARE THE HABITS OF
A LANDSCAPE. THEY ARE
ACTS OF CONSENSUAL
MAKING. IT'S HARD TO
CREATE A FOOTPATH ON
YOUR OWN. . . . LIKE SEA
CHANNELS THAT REQUIRE
REGULAR DREDGING TO
STAY OPEN, PATHS *NEED*
WALKING.

—Robert Macfarlane

INSIST ON A
WILD AND BRAVE STORY

Fear, to a great extent, is born of a story we tell ourselves, and so I chose to tell myself a different story from the one women are told. I decided I was safe. I was strong. I was brave. Nothing could vanquish me. Insisting on this story was a form of mind control, but for the most part, it worked.

—Cheryl Strayed, *Wild*

> As an explorer, Cheryl Strayed is audaciously brave. She treks the rough but beautiful miles of the Pacific Crest Trail, but she also takes an inner walk by surveying the brutal landscape of her own suffering and grief. By adventuring alone on the trail, Cheryl Strayed walks to claim authorship of her own life.

◆ Explore a new footpath, all the while telling yourself a particular story you'd like to be true about yourself. Journal the essence of that story here.

WE DO NOT BELONG TO
THOSE WHO HAVE IDEAS
ONLY AMONG BOOKS, WHEN
STIMULATED BY BOOKS. IT
IS OUR HABIT TO THINK
OUTDOORS—WALKING,
LEAPING, CLIMBING,
DANCING, PREFERABLY ON
LONELY MOUNTAINS OR NEAR
THE SEA WHERE EVEN THE
TRAILS BECOME THOUGHTFUL.

—Friedrich Nietzsche

THE WISDOM OF TRAILS

We tend to glorify trailblazers—those hardy souls who strike out across uncharted territory, both figurative and physical—but followers play an equally important role in creating a trail. They shave off unnecessary bends and brush away obstructions, improving the trail with each trip.

—**Robert Moor,** *On Trails: An Exploration*

> Explorers don't just need paths to walk; paths need explorers to walk upon them so that the pathways remain engraved on the landscape.

◆ Strike out on a trail with your journal and colored pencils.

◆ Recall times in your creative journey when you have been a trailblazer.

◆ Consider other times when your creative endeavors have involved walking a trail blazed by those who came before you.

◆ Write or sketch your responses.

THERE IS
PLEASURE IN THE
PATHLESS WOODS.

—Lord Byron

Devotion

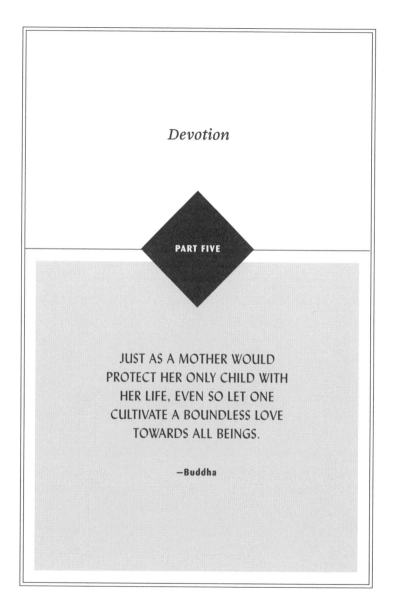

PART FIVE

JUST AS A MOTHER WOULD
PROTECT HER ONLY CHILD WITH
HER LIFE, EVEN SO LET ONE
CULTIVATE A BOUNDLESS LOVE
TOWARDS ALL BEINGS.

—Buddha

So many acts of love, caretaking, and justice have involved walks. As an example, in 1930, Gandhi organized the 241-mile Salt March as a way of nonviolently protesting the British government's salt monopoly in India. Gandhi and his fellow walkers set out on a very long journey afoot in hopes that their steps would call attention to their cause and ultimately improve the conditions of their world.

Once, while on a trip to Ecuador, a group walk gone awry provoked a young stranger to take care of me. For days, rains had pummeled the tin roofs where we were staying, and when the sun finally broke through, a group of us decided to walk with some locals to see the river. The local children seemed thrilled at the prospect of a walk to the river, and they joined our procession through the mud. Not knowing how long the walk would be, I grabbed a two-dollar pair of pink flip-flops I had purchased for times when I needed a quick pair of shoes to walk from place to place.

As we walked through the field, every once in a while, a child would run out of a small house to join our procession. Plodding through that mud in my pink flip-flops became more like stepping in a five-layer chocolate cake. Step after step, I eased my feet out of the mud until, finally, a bright pink flip-flop failed. The strap snapped off as I tried to lift my foot. Everyone behind and ahead of me kept walking. Like a flamingo, I stood on one foot and tried to see if the broken flip-flop could be repaired. It was completely shot. I decided to keep going. I put my bare foot down and let it sink into the mud. I hoisted the foot that still had a shoe on it, and in an instant, the other flip-flop snapped as well. I left it under the inches of deep mud and moved forward on my bare feet.

What else could I do? I tried to enjoy the oozy mud between my toes, but all I could think about were *los parásitos* and snakes. Did I have open cuts on my feet? How could I be so ill-equipped?

Somehow, news I was barefoot began to get out in English and Spanish, up and down the line. A little girl, no older than seven, broke out of line and started running up the hill to a little shack. Someone in our group said it was her house. She came out a couple of seconds later and ran straight to me. In her hands was a pair of plastic shoes, and she put them in my hands with a wide smile. The backs of my feet hung over the ends by three or four inches, but I walked on alongside my new friend.

Though certainly less famous than Gandhi's Salt March, that girl's generous act demonstrated her devotion to making our little world a better place. As I stood on the banks of the wide river we walked to on that day, I promised myself I would try to keep a better watch on strangers and the landscape, to better cultivate love for all beings.

Can cultivating what the Buddha named "a boundless love" for all beings enhance the creative process? Researchers in the Netherlands have found that simply thinking about those we love can make us more focused and more creative. Love literally makes us think differently by activating our creative capacities. As you respond to the following prompts, consider how showing love and compassion for others might be a way to show up for your own creative endeavors. May our own walks lead us to respond to a world in deep need of compassion and care.

WALKING FOR GOOD

In an essay titled "Stepping Out," David Sedaris recounts how he turned an obsession with earning steps on his Fitbit into the practice of picking up trash in the beautiful area of England where he lives. Sedaris shines light on a serious point: that walking can be used not only to improve an individual's well-being, sense of place, and attention, but it can also be a way of taking care of others and inspiring acts of devotion.

◆ Set out on a long walk in your neighborhood, noticing anything affecting the buildings or the landscape that might need caretaking.

◆ Journal about how mindful pursuits might be turned into a devotional practice that can improve the conditions of your immediate community.

IT'S NO USE WALKING
ANYWHERE TO PREACH
UNLESS OUR WALKING IS
OUR PREACHING.

—Saint Francis of Assisi

I WILL NOT LET
ANYONE WALK
THROUGH MY MIND
WITH THEIR
DIRTY FEET.

—attributed to
Mahatma Gandhi

PLANETWALKER

A lot of time we find ourselves in this wonderful place where we've gotten to but there's another place we have to go, and so we have to leave behind the security of who we've become and go to the place of who we are becoming.

—John Francis

After seeing two oil tankers collide in the San Francisco Bay in a disastrous oil spill in 1971, twenty-five-year-old John Francis walked across the United States and part of South America in an act of devotion for the environment. For seventeen of the years he was walking, Francis stopped talking entirely. He did so because he felt he was inhibiting authentic communication. He eventually created an organization, Planetwalk, that sponsors walks around the world aimed at bringing attention to environmental education and responsibility.

◆ Emulate Francis on your walk today. Be silent and listen to your surroundings.

◆ What does it mean to be devoted to our environment?

LOVE LETTER

I have two luxuries to brood over in my walks, your loveliness and the hour of my death. O that I could have possession of them both in the same minute.

—John Keats

◆ Walk, composing a love letter as you go along the way. The love letter can be intended for a romantic partner, a dear friend, a historical figure, a child, a parent—anyone.

WE SHALL
NOT CEASE
FROM
EXPLORATION,
AND THE END
OF ALL OUR
EXPLORING
WILL BE TO

ARRIVE WHERE WE STARTED AND KNOW THE PLACE FOR THE FIRST TIME.

—T. S. ELIOT

COMMEMORATION

I once attended a memorial service unlike any I had
ever attended: a walk around a small lake. We were
there to remember a friend who walked that loop
regularly with her dog, and as we silently processed
along the path, we kept our friend in mind. Instead
of black, the mourners donned comfortable shoes and
clothes; instead of a gilded ceiling, we gazed up to see
a vivid blue afternoon sky.

◆ Walk a path in commemoration of a person or persons you
love.

◆ As you walk, take deep breaths in thanksgiving for the steps
they walked on this earth.

◆ Stop several times along the path to journal, sketch, or create
in their honor.

THERE IS NO EASY WALK
TO FREEDOM ANYWHERE,
AND MANY OF US WILL
HAVE TO PASS THROUGH
THE VALLEY OF THE
SHADOW OF DEATH
AGAIN AND AGAIN
BEFORE WE REACH THE
MOUNTAINTOP OF OUR
DESIRES.

—Nelson Mandela

MARCH

The universe is with us. Walk together, children. Don't get weary.

—John Lewis, *March*

> On March 7, 1965, John Lewis and about six hundred
> other African Americans set off on a walk—a march
> for civil rights—from Selma, Alabama, to the state
> capital of Montgomery. That day became known as
> Bloody Sunday, and about a week later, President
> Johnson called the Selma march "a turning point in
> man's unending search for freedom."

◆ Walk a route that includes a bridge, if possible, and marvel
at the symbolism of crossings. Consider this: Is there a cause
for which you'd march? Have you already taken to the streets
for justice, freedom, or peace?

◆ Sketch a series of captioned images—like a comic strip—
detailing your response here.

IF YOU HEAR THE DOGS,
KEEP GOING. IF YOU SEE
THE TORCHES IN THE
WOODS, KEEP GOING. IF
THERE'S SHOUTING AFTER
YOU, KEEP GOING. DON'T
EVER STOP. KEEP GOING.
IF YOU WANT A TASTE OF
FREEDOM, KEEP GOING.

—Harriet Tubman

CREATING AS A CITIZEN

The exercise of democracy begins as exercise, as walking around, becoming familiar with the streets, comfortable with strangers, able to imagine your own body as powerful and expressive rather than a pawn. People who are at home in their civic space preserve the power to protest and revolt, whereas those who have been sequestered into private space do not.

—**Rebecca Solnit,** "Democracy Should Be Exercised Regularly, on Foot"

> Rebecca Solnit has written about the importance of having a tangible life as a citizen, not just a life as a consumer, "screened from solidarity with strangers and increasingly afraid or even unable to imagine acting in public." Walking is essential to the human right to freely assemble or associate.

◆ Walk freely in a public place today and reflect on the strangers you encounter, considering how, like you, they are citizens of somewhere.

◆ Reflect on the space you encounter as civic space, not someone's private property.

DESIRE LINES

For urban designers, studying a city's "desire lines"—
the paths that emerge as a result of pedestrians'
shortcuts—is particularly edifying.

◆ As you walk today, pay particular attention to the design of the
streets you walk. Take note of any desire lines you encounter
or create.

◆ Consider the paths you walk frequently, thinking about where
or why you take shortcuts. Reflect on a time when trusting
your own intuition proved to be more fruitful than sticking to
someone else's path.

PEACE PILGRIM

What would it take for all humans to be able to walk in a peaceful world? Mildred Lisette Norman Ryder, known as "Peace Pilgrim," walked across North America for almost three decades in honor of this question. She made the decision to begin walking for peace in 1938, and traveled afoot more than twenty-five thousand miles, vowing to "remain a wanderer until mankind has learned the way of peace, walking until given shelter and fasting until given food."

◆ As you walk and journal today, reflect on human beings who have walked away from a "normal" life because they were deeply devoted to a particular cause—relief from suffering, the pursuit of beauty or nonviolence, devotion to silent prayer or meditation, or a search for inner wisdom.

THE CREATIVE WALKING CHALLENGE

I don't know what inspiration is. But when it comes I hope it finds me working.

—attributed to Pablo Picasso

We often imagine that creative work emerges suddenly and mysteriously following a lightning bolt of inspiration. And sometimes it does! But more often than not, creative work is a result of devotion, intention, resolve, and consistency.

For the next thirty days, challenge yourself to walk every day and to set aside time for an artistic endeavor.

◆ At the same time each day, walk somewhere you can stretch your legs and let your imagination soar.

◆ Develop the habit of settling down at your desk or in your studio as soon as your walk ends. Or if it works better for you, pause at points along the path to do creative work.

◆ Keep track of your thirty-day challenge and reflect on this nourishing new habit you're forming.

FILL YOUR PAPER
WITH THE BREATHINGS OF
YOUR HEART.

—William Wordsworth

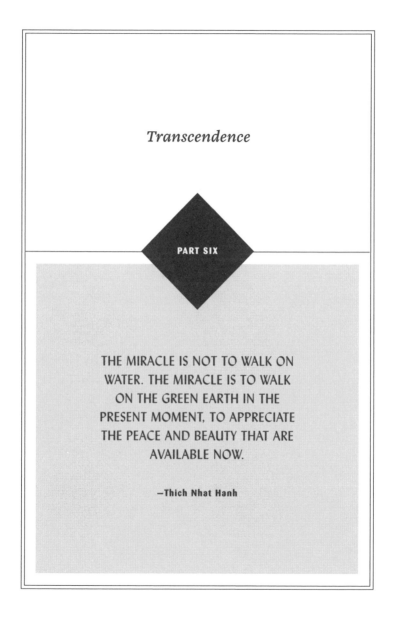

Transcendence

PART SIX

THE MIRACLE IS NOT TO WALK ON
WATER. THE MIRACLE IS TO WALK
ON THE GREEN EARTH IN THE
PRESENT MOMENT, TO APPRECIATE
THE PEACE AND BEAUTY THAT ARE
AVAILABLE NOW.

—Thich Nhat Hanh

Just as human beings long to create, human beings hunger for spiritual experiences that transcend the physical world; surely this is why humans have invented symbols like thresholds, gates, and—my personal favorite—labyrinths. The labyrinth is an ancient tool found in cultures across time and space. Think of a labyrinth as a symbolic map human beings have created to marry the physical and the spiritual. Unlike mazes, which have multiple exits and entrances, all labyrinths have one path that winds back to the center. Some have said that the point of a maze is to find its center, and the point of a labyrinth is to find your center. The labyrinth represents an archetypal path for humans, a path that has been traveled before you by millions of people from different times and cultures.

As a child, I first walked a labyrinth at summer camp. On the concrete floor of the camp's pavilion, I took very slow steps on my dirty bare feet through the path where a labyrinth had been painted. I remember being surprised at how long it took to reach the center. Earlier this year, I watched my young son approach the same labyrinth on his own dirty bare feet; I smiled as he walked in wonder and with a little bit of trepidation. Over many years, I have sought out labyrinths, walking them in my bare feet on cold cathedral floors or through dewy leaves of grass. What you do when you finally reach the center of the labyrinth is completely up to you; there is no wrong way to approach your walk. You can be silent, pray, or meditate; you can write or paint; you can listen to music; you can assume a yoga pose, feel the breeze, or gaze upon a tree.

A labyrinth imprints a small metaphorical walk on the earth with one singular purpose: to allow human beings a bit of time and space to transcend the everydayness of their lives. This transcendence is both a beginning and an ending. Once we reach the labyrinth's conclusion point, we are launched forward and offered an eloquent lesson for living on this earth: my walk, like yours, will end someday. My being will cross a threshold and transcend from the physical.

When I dream of what I can leave behind as an offering to the world, I think of my children, and the loving-kindness that I hope I have shown for them, my husband, family, friends, students—even my dogs. I think of my creative work, and I remember that many throughout time have created so that they may leave their art behind as a way of achieving immortality. But also, I dream of leaving behind a simple and beautiful labyrinth, a transcendent path for others who come after me to walk in search of peace, contemplation, and inspiration.

As you approach the walks and prompts in this final section of *Afoot and Lighthearted,* consider how walks have an unparalleled ability to get us out of our own heads, helping us transcend our finite human problems and conditions. Walks can place us at thresholds of the sacred, transforming us from busy professionals into pilgrims. Or perhaps our walks can help dissolve the borders between the sacred and the ordinary entirely.

IF A MAN
WISHES
TO BE SURE
OF THE
ROAD HE
TREADS
ON,

HE MUST CLOSE HIS EYES AND WALK IN THE DARK.

—SAINT JOHN OF THE CROSS

SKYWARD

This is love: to fly toward a secret sky, to cause a hundred veils to fall each moment. First to let go of life. Finally, to take a step without feet.

—Rumi, *Diwan-e Shams-e Tabrizi*

◆ Many consider drawing to be a form of contemplation
   and communion connecting the spiritual and physical realms.
   Take a walk with your eyes turned skyward, then stop to
   sketch what you see.

WHAT DOES THE LORD
REQUIRE OF YOU BUT TO
DO JUSTICE, AND
TO LOVE KINDNESS, AND
TO WALK HUMBLY WITH
YOUR GOD?

—Micah 6:8

THE ART OF SAUNTERING

I have met with but one or two persons in the course of my life who understood the art of Walking, that is, of taking walks—who had a genius, so to speak, for *sauntering*. . . . Some, however, would derive the word from *sans terre*, without land or a home, which, therefore, in the good sense, will mean, having no particular home, but equally at home everywhere. For this is the secret of successful sauntering.

—Henry David Thoreau

Sauntering is a human art practiced by those who understand that walking can be a way to transcend the humdrum of everyday life by finding a home in our inherent wildness and holiness.

◆ Make time to take a long saunter. As you walk, make a mindful attempt to notice all that surrounds you in every step you take. Capture your experience in words or in a drawing.

THE MOON AND JUPITER SIDE BY SIDE
LAST NIGHT STEMMED THE SEA OF
CLOUDS AND PLIED THEIR VOYAGE IN
CONVOY THROUGH THE SUBLIME DEEP
AS I WALKED THE OLD AND DUSTY ROAD.
THE SNOW AND THE ENCHANTMENT OF
THE MOONLIGHT MAKE ALL LANDSCAPES
ALIKE, AND THE ROAD THAT IS SO
TEDIOUS AND HOMELY THAT I NEVER
TAKE IT BY DAY—BY NIGHT IT IS ITALY
OR PALMYRA. IN THESE DIVINE
PLEASURES PERMITTED TO ME OF WALKS
IN THE JUNE NIGHT UNDER MOON AND
STARS, I CAN PUT MY LIFE AS A FACT
BEFORE ME AND STAND ALOOF FROM ITS
HONOR AND SHAME.

—the Journals of Ralph Waldo Emerson,
June 28, 1838

HAIBUN

The moon and sun are eternal travelers. Even the years wander on. . . .
I have been drawn by windblown clouds into dreams of a lifetime of
wandering.

—Matsuo Bashō, "The Narrow Road to the Interior"

> In the late seventeenth century, the Japanese poet
> Bashō began taking months-long journeys on foot.
> He invented *haibun*, a poetic form that immortalizes
> a journey by using prose and poetry. Follow in
> Bashō's footsteps on your walk by creating a *haibun*
> in your journal. The formula is fairly straightforward.

◆ First, focus on the external: use imagistic prose to describe
   what you observe outside yourself on your walk.

◆ Second, create a haiku to describe what you observe inside
   yourself on your walk.

◆ Repeat the process by interlacing prose and haiku.

WALKING THE LABYRINTH

The labyrinth offers us the possibility of being real creatures in symbolic space. . . . In such spaces as the labyrinth we cross over; we are really travelling, even if the destination is only symbolic.

—**Rebecca Solnit,** *Wanderlust*

> Visit labyrinthlocator.com, a directory of labyrinths around the world. If you can, visit the nearest labyrinth. If not, you can view a regular walking route as a labyrinthine journey in its own right.

◆ Take off your shoes, in reverence for the labyrinth as a sacred space. Pause at the entrance and reflect on how your walk might help with a particular question you have or a creative endeavor you are undertaking.

◆ As you walk toward the center of the labyrinth, breathe, relax, and consider the internal journey you're taking.

◆ When you reach the center, stop for a while, perhaps sitting in meditation or prayer. When you are ready, begin to walk the path back to where you began.

◆ Sit nearby, and reflect on your journey.

WALKING IS THE GREAT
ADVENTURE, THE FIRST
MEDITATION, A PRACTICE
OF HEARTINESS AND SOUL
PRIMARY TO HUMANKIND.
WALKING IS THE EXACT
BALANCE BETWEEN SPIRIT
AND HUMILITY.

—Gary Snyder

PILGRIMS

Pilgrims are poets who create by taking journeys.

—H. Richard Niebuhr, quoted in Sue Monk Kidd and Ann Kidd
Taylor's *Traveling with Pomegranates*

> A pilgrimage is a kind of transitional state—an
> "in-betweenness"—because on pilgrimage, you are
> literally in the middle of one place and another. On
> a pilgrimage, you bring your own inner world to the
> physical world. Step by step, pilgrims journey across
> the landscape to search for healing, to pay homage
> to a person or place, or to pursue a path toward
> enlightenment.

◆ If you were to take the journey of a pilgrimage, where might
you go? Who might go with you? What would you be sure to
take, and what would you be sure to leave behind?

◆ List the spiritual or creative needs that might propel you on
such a journey.

CERTAINLY THERE IS WITHIN
EACH OF US A SELF THAT
IS NEITHER A CHILD,
NOR A SERVANT OF THE
HOURS. IT IS A THIRD SELF,
OCCASIONAL IN SOME
OF US, TYRANT IN
OTHERS. THIS SELF IS OUT
OF LOVE WITH THE
ORDINARY; IT IS OUT OF
LOVE WITH TIME. IT HAS
A HUNGER FOR ETERNITY.

—Mary Oliver, *Upstream*

PORTALS

In Japan, a *torii* is a gate marking an opening to
a sacred space. *Torii* show walkers the path and
demarcate the thresholds between sacred and
ordinary spaces; they are wide-open gates, and their
openness seems to suggest that the sacred permeates
the walker's path wherever she or he wanders.

◆ Walk to a hallowed space, a place either you or others
consider to be sacred. Sketch the threshold that marks the
opening of that space.

◆ Journal about portals. Portals signal arrivals and departures;
they mark beginnings and endings. What do the portals
on your path signal to you? Do you believe there are lines
between sacred and ordinary spaces? Or do you feel that
all space is sacred?

WITH BEAUTY BEFORE ME,
MAY I WALK

WITH BEAUTY BEHIND ME,
MAY I WALK

WITH BEAUTY ABOVE ME,
MAY I WALK

WITH BEAUTY BELOW ME,
MAY I WALK

WITH BEAUTY ALL AROUND ME,
MAY I WALK

WANDERING ON THE TRAIL OF BEAUTY,
MAY I WALK.

—Navajo walking meditation

WALKING MEDITATION II

Walk as if you are kissing the Earth with your feet.

—Thich Nhat Hanh, *Peace Is Every Step*

Walking meditation is defined on page 104. Practice walking meditation once again by bringing your attention and awareness to the soles of your feet, to the here and now. As you meditate, practice a pace that is slightly slower than your normal walking pace, and focus your attention on the soles of your feet as you did before. But this time, with each footstep, imagine you are fusing your own creative energy with the creative energy of the earth.

◆ After a time, sit down with your journal and reflect on energy, attention, and awareness. Have you kissed the earth with your feet?

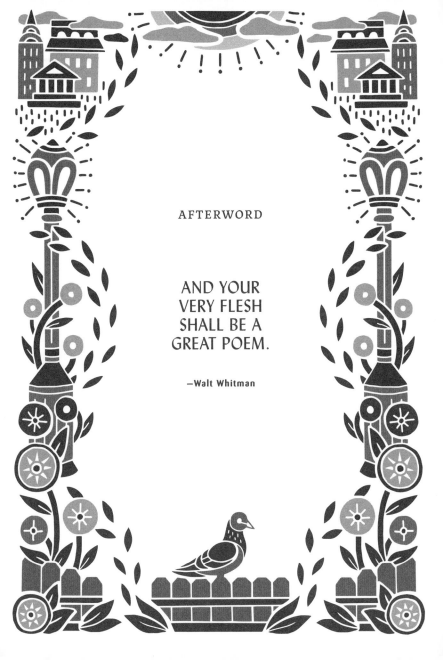

AFTERWORD

AND YOUR
VERY FLESH
SHALL BE A
GREAT POEM.

—Walt Whitman

Evidence suggests that around six million years ago, the first human beings began walking on two legs, a profound development that initially helped them take advantage of their habitats and gradually helped them become creators. A quintessential human activity, walking offers powerful physical, mental, and spiritual benefits; as we think about our societies and the policies that govern them, we would do well to design communities that support walkers. In our twenty-first-century lives, barriers to walking certainly exist. Automobiles, lighting, crime, pollution, lack of sidewalks and green spaces, and insufficient access to public transportation deter walkers from walking. Walking is a distinctly human characteristic and access to safe, walkable communities should be a human right.

For so many people throughout space and time, a walk has been a productive, vibrant way to step away from everyday life and gain a refreshed perspective. Aristotle and the peripatetic philosophers walked as a way to inquire philosophically and to educate others. In preparation for his ministry, Jesus walked through the desert for forty days. The Buddha walked for years before he found enlightenment. Indigenous Australians memorized and passed down songlines to trace and communicate invisible pathways across the continent, marking their ancestors' routes and guiding them across a vast continent. Walkers have walked to gain a sense of place, to improve well-being, to harness attention, to cultivate awareness, to gain new experiences, to explore new territories, to march for freedom, and to express care and devotion for others.

I have longed to create from the time I was aware of such a thing called creativity; most likely, I have hungered to be creative as long as I have been able to walk. I have observed my children's longing to be creators evolve alongside their aptitude as walkers. My seven-year-old is a yarn spinner, a dimpled storyteller who specializes in comedy and loves to use words to create a scene that will delight his audience. Since my five-year-old son began talking, he has told anyone who will listen, "When I grow up I want to be an artist-giant," meaning a grown-up who paints pictures. I don't think we are alone; I believe that a longing to create is part of what it means to be human.

As you have walked and worked from the prompts in *Afoot and Lighthearted,* I hope you experienced how walking can unleash creativity and mindfulness. Creativity does not just come from some fickle well hidden inside the self that sometimes is bone-dry and sometimes flows abundantly; mindfulness is inexorably linked up with the body, with movement, with love, and with the natural world. Likewise, "the walk" is not simply a shopworn cliché for the journey; walking is willingly showing up for the world, exploring in spite of fears, and being present in spite of a never-ending cavalcade of distractions that await us. May we all show up for this magnificent world and its inhabitants as we walk, kissing the very earth with our footsteps.

FOR FURTHER READING

(listed by author's last name)

Wendell Berry, *It All Turns on Affection: The Jefferson Lecture & Other Essays*

Nicholas Carr, *The Shallows: What the Internet Is Doing to Our Brains*

Shelley Carson, *Your Creative Brain*

Bruce Chatwin, *The Songlines*

Mason Currey, *Daily Rituals: How Artists Work*

Michel de Certeau, *The Practice of Everyday Life* (see Part III: Spatial Practices)

Annie Dillard, *Pilgrim at Tinker Creek* and *The Writing Life*

Elizabeth Gilbert, *Big Magic: Creative Living Beyond Fear*

Frédéric Gros, *A Philosophy of Walking*

David George Haskell, *The Forest Unseen: A Year's Watch in Nature*

Alexandra Horowitz, *On Looking: Eleven Walks with Expert Eyes*

Jon Kabat-Zinn, *Full Catastrophe Living* and *Wherever You Go, There You Are*

Sue Monk Kidd and Ann Kidd Taylor, *Traveling with Pomegranates: A Mother and Daughter Journey to the Sacred Places of Greece, Turkey, and France*

John Lewis, *March*

Dr. Qing Li, *Forest Bathing: How Trees Can Help You Find Health and Happiness*

Richard Louv, *Last Child in the Woods: Saving Our Children from Nature-Deficit Disorder*

Robert Macfarlane, *The Old Ways: A Journey on Foot*

Robert Moor, *On Trails: An Exploration*

Mary Oliver, *Collected Poems* and *Upstream*

Adrienne Rich, *Diving into the Wreck*

Bertrand Russell, *In Praise of Idleness*

Rebecca Solnit, *Wanderlust*

Cheryl Strayed, *Wild*

Thich Nhat Hanh, *Peace Is Every Step: The Path of Mindfulness in Everyday Life*

Henry David Thoreau, "Walking"

Walt Whitman, *Leaves of Grass*

Florence Williams, *The Nature Fix: Why Nature Makes Us Happier, Healthier, and More Creative*

The Walker's Literary Companion (eds. Roger Gilbert, Jeffrey Robinson, and Anne Wallace)

GRATITUDE

So many delightful and compassionate companions, family members, friends, and students walk beside me. Colleagues in the field of writing studies and at Belmont University have been particularly encouraging as I have learned and taught about walking and creativity over the years, especially Mary Lou Odom, John Duffy, Catherine Prendergast, Amy Hodges Hamilton, Sarah Blomeley, Jason Lovvorn, Charmion Gustke, Lauren Lunsford, Andrea Stover, Douglas Murray, Annette Sisson, John Paine, Cynthia Cox, Marnie Vanden Noven, and Marcia McDonald, who was the first believer in this project. I am particularly grateful to Holly Huddleston and the hundreds of students who have passed through our wellness and writing learning communities. The methods and creative approaches of Deborah Brandt, Andrea Lunsford, and Cheryl Glenn illuminate my path.

The Porch Writers' Collective (Katie McDougall and Susannah Felts), Parnassus Books (Sissy Gardner and Mary Laura Philpott), and my dear friends Tallu Quinn, Holly McCathren, Katha Raulston, Katy Varney, Ellen Register, Becca Stevens, and Liz Van Hoose offered sanctuary, guidance, and wonderful ideas.

Sara Neville and the team at Clarkson Potter, including Lindley Boegehold, Danielle Deschenes, Kevin Garcia, and Patricia Shaw, and our wonderful illustrator, Caitlin Keegan, have been incredibly wonderful to work with as we have brought *Afoot and Lighthearted* to life. And the brilliant advice of my kind friend and literary agent Anna Knutson Geller of Write View exists on every page of this book. Creating this book alongside Anna has been such a pleasure.

Thank you to the Hillsboro-West End Neighborhood Association and the leaders of Nashville for their recent enlightened decision to create the first walking districts in our city. My hope is that more walking districts will be created across the world to respect and celebrate the delights and benefits of traveling afoot.

My family—especially Sharon and Floyd Smith, Kelly Smith Trimble, and Patricia Lockett— not only helped me to learn how to walk when I was a child but also surrounded me with supportive roots that would enable me to experiment, to take risks, to persist, and to live a creative life. My sister Kelly is the finest reader and writer I know. This book is dedicated to my husband, Ben, and our children, Henry and Peter, whose love encourages every step I take.

ABOUT THE AUTHOR

BONNIE SMITH WHITEHOUSE, a professor of English at Belmont University, specializes in the flourishing field of writing studies. She lives in a walking district in Nashville, Tennessee, with her husband, Ben; their sons, Henry and Peter; and their dogs, Teddy and Franklin.